Let's Explore

GW00870146

Growing up

by Henry Pluckrose

W

FRANKLIN WATTS

NEW YORK • LONDON • SYDNEY

Author's note

This book is one of a series which has been designed to encourage young readers to think about the everyday concepts that form part of their world. The text and photographs complement each other, and both elements combine to provide starting points for discussion. Although each book is complete in itself, each title links closely with others in the set, so presenting an ideal platform for learning.

I have consciously avoided 'writing down' to my readers. Young children like to know the 'real' words for things, and are better able to express themselves when they can use correct terms with confidence.

Young children learn from the experiences they share with adults around them. The child offers his or her ideas which are then developed and extended through the adult. The books in this series are a means for the child and adult to share informal talk, photographs and text, and the ideas which accompany them.

One particular element merits comment. Information books are also reading books. Like a successful story book, an effective information book will be turned to again and again. As children develop, their appreciation of the significance of fact develops too. The young child who asks 'Where did I come from, Mummy?' may subsequently and more provocatively ask, 'How did Daddy help you make me?' Thoughts take time to generate. Hopefully books like those in this series provide the momentum for this.

Henry Pluckrose

Contents

When you were a baby,
you were quite helpless.
You needed loving parents
to care for you, to feed you,
to watch over you while you slept.

The food you ate,
milk and cheese,
vegetables and fruit,
fish and meat,
helped you to grow
taller and stronger.

Soon, you began to move around.
You could crawl, stand up,
and even walk.

9

When you were a baby,
the first sounds you made
were of laughter and tears.
Now you can talk.
How did you learn?

As you grew up,
you learned new things.
Now, you can walk and run,
skip and climb.

But although you are getting bigger, you are still quite small.

It is not always easy being small.

Chairs are too big,

door handles are too high.

Reaching the light is impossible.

What things do you

find it hard to do?

Growing up is marked
with lots of special days,
like birthdays and other
family celebrations.

Growing up means
doing things for the first time.
Can you remember the first time
you played in the snow?
Or the first time you saw the sea?
What other first times
can you remember?

As you get older,
you learn to read books,
to count and to use a computer.

You learn to use
your hands to do things.
You can write your name.
You can paint a picture.
What other things
do you use your hands for?

You begin to do things
with your friends.
You learn to play football,
ride a pony, ride a bike
and swim in a pool.

Growing up is not all fun.

Everybody has secret fears.

Some people are frightened of spiders.

Other people are frightened of
seeing shadows in the moonlight.

Do you have any secret fears?

One day, you will be a grown-up.
You might have children
of your own.
Then you can tell them
all about growing up.

Index

First published in 1999 by
Franklin Watts
96 Leonard Street
London
EC2A 4XD

Franklin Watts Australia
14 Mars Road
Lane Cove
NSW 2066

Copyright © Franklin Watts 1999

ISBN 0 7496 3465 0

Dewey Decimal
Classification Number 612

A CIP catalogue record for this book is
available from the British Library

Series editor: Louise John
Series designer: Jason Anscomb

Printed in Hong Kong

Picture Credits:
Steve Shott Photography pp. 8, 9, 14, 16, 22,
cover and title page; Bubbles pp. 4 (Lupe
Cunha), 11 (Loisjoy Thurstun), 12 (Pauline
Cutler), 19 (Jennie Woodcock), 20 (Ian
West), 28 (Ian West), 31 (Loisjoy Thurstun);
The Image Bank p. 7 (Jeff Cadge); Robert
Harding pp. 25 (Liaison Int.), 27 (Jeff
Greenberg).